PIANO · VOCAL · GUITAR

TOP HITS OF
2020

ISBN 978-1-70511-120-8

HAL•LEONARD®

7777 W. BLUEMOUND RD. P.O. BOX 13819 MILWAUKEE, WI 53213

Visit Hal Leonard Online at
www.halleonard.com

Contact us:
Hal Leonard
7777 West Bluemound Road
Milwaukee, WI 53213
Email: info@halleonard.com

In Europe, contact:
Hal Leonard Europe Limited
42 Wigmore Street
Marylebone, London, W1U 2RN
Email: info@halleonardeurope.com

In Australia, contact:
Hal Leonard Australia Pty. Ltd.
4 Lentara Court
Cheltenham, Victoria, 3192 Australia
Email: info@halleonard.com.au

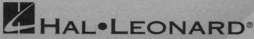

ADORE YOU

Words and Music by HARRY STYLES,
THOMAS HULL, TYLER JOHNSON
and AMY ALLEN

I'd walk through fi-re for you. Just let me a-dore you.

you. Oh, hon-ey.

Just let me a-dore you.

you like it's the on-ly thing I'll ev-er do.

BREAK MY HEART

Words and Music by DUA LIPA,
ANDREW FARRISS, MICHAEL HUTCHENCE,
JORDAN JOHNSON, ANDREW WOTMAN,
STEFAN JOHNSON and ALI TAMPOSI

BE KIND

Words and Music by ASHLEY FRANGIPANE,
MARSHMELLO, AMY ALLEN,
GIAN STONE and FREDDY WEXLER

Wan-na be-lieve, wan-na be-lieve that you don't have a bad bone in your bod-y. But the bruis-es on your e-go make you go wild, wild, wild, yeah.

Wan-na be-lieve, wan-na be-lieve that e-ven when you're stone cold, you're sor-

BEFORE YOU GO

Words and Music by LEWIS CAPALDI,
BENJAMIN KOHN, PETER KELLEHER,
THOMAS BARNES and PHILIP PLESTED

I fell by the way-side, ___ like ev'-ry-one else.
Was nev-er the right time ___ when-ev-er you called.

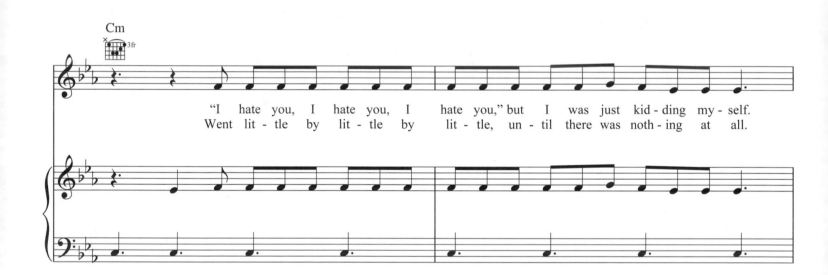

"I hate you, I hate you, I hate you," but I was just kid-ding my-self.
Went lit-tle by lit-tle by lit-tle, un-til there was noth-ing at all.

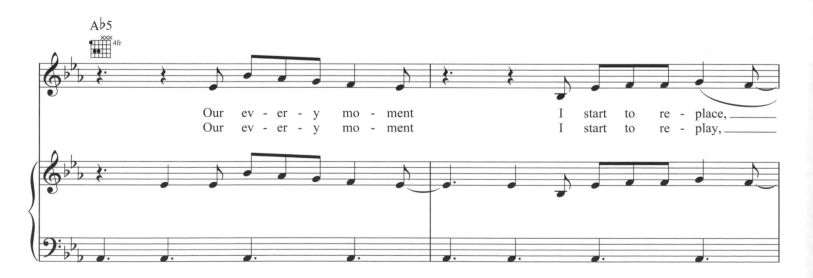

Our ev-er-y mo-ment I start to re-place, ___
Our ev-er-y mo-ment I start to re-play, ___

BETTER DAYS

Words and Music by RYAN TEDDER,
BRENT KUTZLE and JOHN NATHANIEL

Oh, I know that there'll be bet- ter days. __

Oh, that sun-shine 'bout to come my way. __ May we nev-er, ev-er shed an-oth-er

tear for to- day, _____ 'cause, oh, I know that there'll be bet- ter days. _ Wak-ing

CARDIGAN

Words and Music by TAYLOR SWIFT
and AARON DESSNER

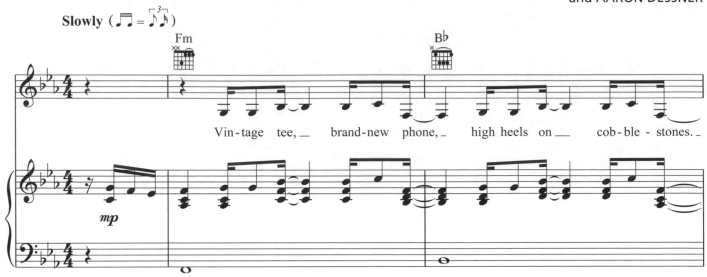

Vin-tage tee,_ brand-new phone,_ high heels on_ cob-ble-stones.

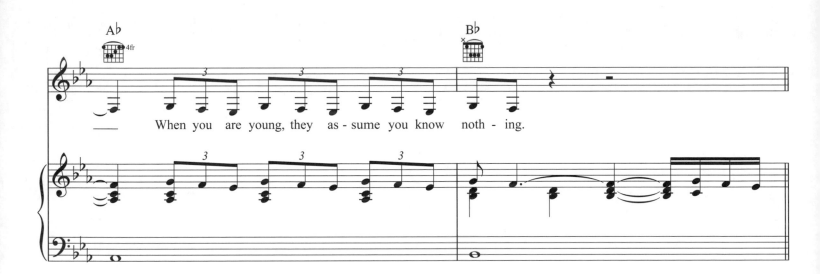

_ When you are young, they as-sume you know noth-ing.

Se-quin smile,_ black lip-stick,_ sen-su-al_ pol-i-tics.
A friend to all_ is a friend to none. Chase two girls,_ lose the one._

DAISIES

Words and Music by KATY PERRY,
MICHAEL POLLACK, JON BELLION,
JORDAN JOHNSON, JACOB KASHER HINDLIN
and STEFAN JOHNSON

Lyrics:
Told them your dreams and they all started laughing.
I guess you're out of your mind till it actually happens.

When did we all stop believing in magic?
Why did we put all our hopes in a box in the attic?

*Recorded a half step lower.

IN YOUR EYES

Words and Music by ABEL TESFAYE,
MAX MARTIN, OSCAR HOLTER
and AHMAD BALSHE

I DARE YOU

Words and Music by BENJAMIN WEST,
JEFFREY GITELMAN, NATALIE HEMBY,
LAURA VELTZ and JESSE SHATKIN

Moderately

mf

There's a wolf that preys on a world that strays so ____
full of hope tryin' to stay a-float, tryin' to

far from the gar-den.
save one an-oth-er.

And just like your __ own, ev-'ry
Peo-ple let you __ drown 'cause they

heart you __ know seems __ cold and __ hard-ened.
don't know __ how to __ stay a-bove __ wa-ter.

You
When

I'M READY

Words and Music by SAM SMITH,
DEMITRIA LOVATO, SAVAN KOTECHA,
ANDERS PETER SVENSSON and ILYA SALMANZADEH

Female sings 2nd time 8vb.

LEVEL OF CONCERN

Words and Music by
TYLER JOSEPH

Pan - ic on the brink. World ___ has gone in - sane. Things ___
Pan - ic on the brink. Mi - chael's gone in - sane. Ju -

___ are start - ing to get heav - y. I
- lie starts to make you nerv - ous. I don't real - ly

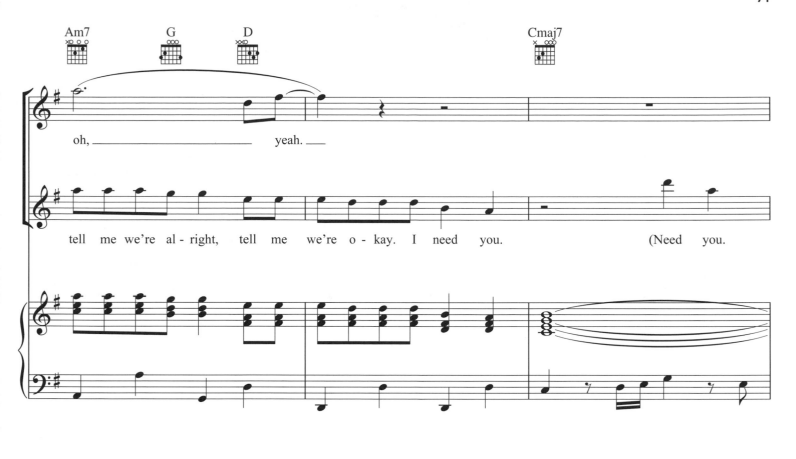

oh, _____ yeah. ___

tell me we're al-right, tell me we're o-kay. I need you. (Need you.

Tell me.   Need you.   Tell me.)

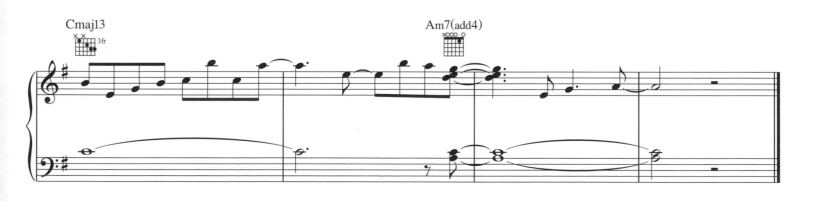

MANIAC

Words and Music by CONAN GRAY
and DANIEL NIGRO

NO TIME TO DIE

from NO TIME TO DIE

Words and Music by BILLIE EILISH O'CONNELL
and FINNEAS O'CONNELL

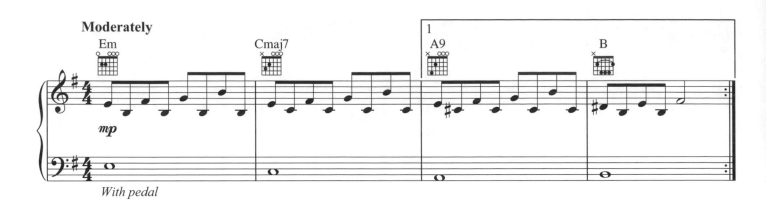

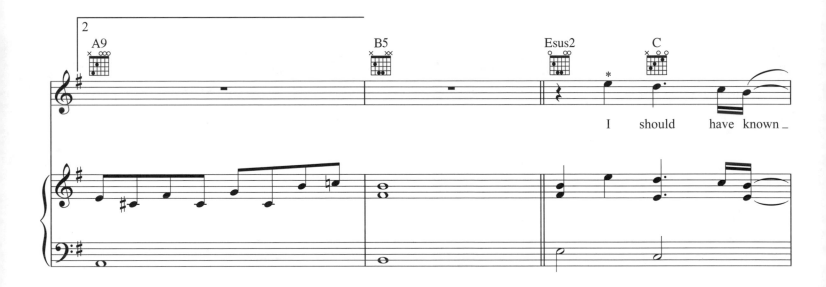

I should have known _

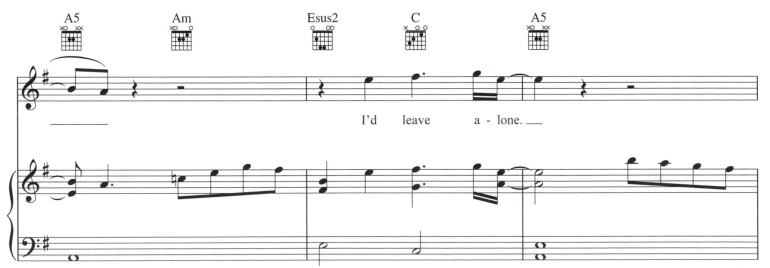

I'd leave a - lone. _

Vocal written one octave higher than sung.

NOBODY'S LOVE

Words and Music by ADAM LEVINE,
NIJA CHARLES, JORDAN JOHNSON,
JACOB KASHER HINDLIN, STEFAN JOHNSON,
RYAN OGREN, MICHAEL POLLACK,
BRANDON HAMLIN, KAREEN LOMAX
and ROSINA RUSSELL

Moderately

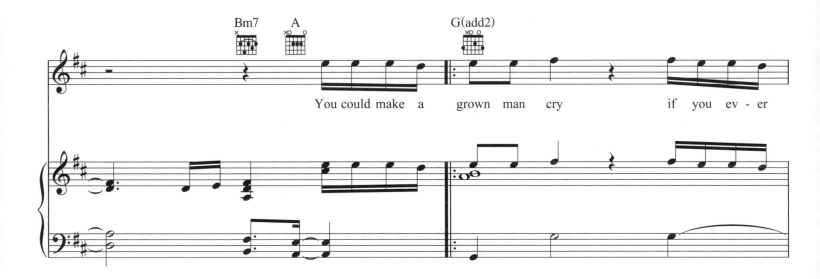

You could make a grown man cry if you ev- er

said good- bye. Nev- er let you go, _____ I.

* Recorded a half step lower.

RAIN ON ME

Words and Music by STEFANI GERMANOTTA,
MARTIN BRESSO, MICHAEL TUCKER,
RAMI YACOUB, ARIANA GRANDE,
NIJA CHARLES and MATTHEW BURNS

THE OTHER SIDE
from TROLLS WORLD TOUR

Words and Music by JUSTIN TIMBERLAKE,
SOLANA IMANI ROWE, MAX MARTIN,
SARAH AARONS and LUDWIG GÖRANSSON

SAY SO

Words and Music by LUKASZ GOTTWALD,
AMALA RATNA DLAMINI, YETI BEATS
and LYDIA ASRAT

Moderately fast

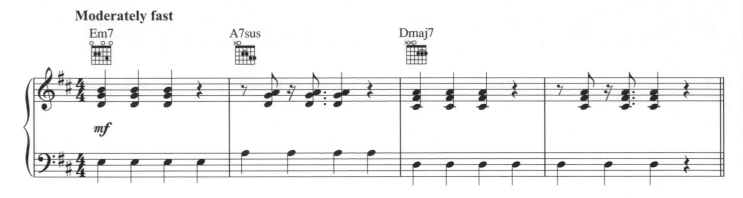

Day to night to morn-ing, keep-ing me in the mo-ment. I'd let you, had I known it. Why

don't you say so? Did-n't e-ven no-tice, no punch-es left to roll with. You

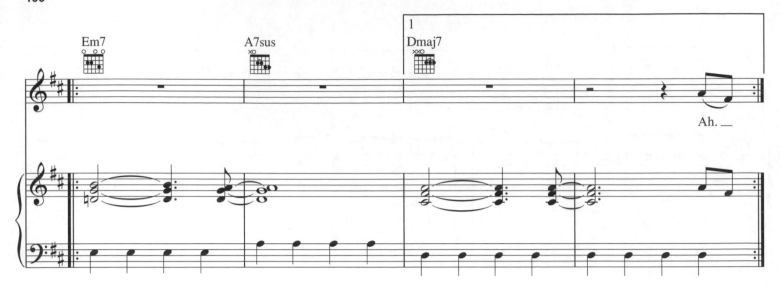

Ah. __

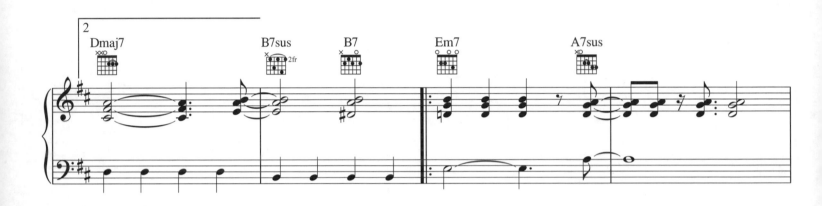

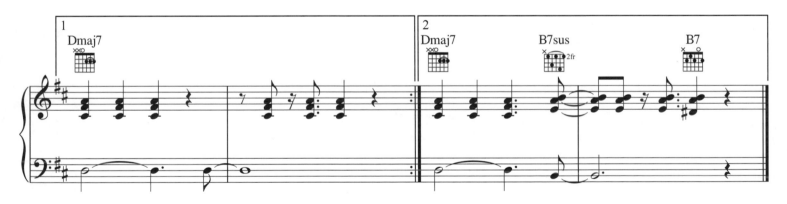

Additional Lyrics

Rap: Let me check my chest, my breath right quick. (Ha.)
He ain't never seen it in a dress like this.
Ah, he ain't never even been impressed like this.
Prob'ly why I got him quiet on the set, like, zip.

Like it, love it, need it bad.
Take it, own it, steal it fast.
Boy, stop playing: grab my ass.

Shut it, save it, keep it pushing.
Why you beating 'round the bush,
And knowing you want all this woman?

All of them bitches hating I have you with me.
All of my niggas saying you mad committed.
Realer than anybody you had, and pretty.
All of the body-ody, the ass and titties.

WHAT A MAN GOTTA DO

Words and Music by NICK JONAS,
JOSEPH JONAS, KEVIN JONAS,
RYAN TEDDER, JESSICA AGOMBAR
and DAVID STEWART

Energetic Pop Rock

Caught my heart ___ a - bout one, two times, don't need to ques - tion the rea - son I'm yours,
You ain't tryin' ___ to be wast - ing time on stu - pid peo - ple and cheap lines, I'm sure,

I'm yours. _____ I'd
I'm sure. _____ So, I'd

A

move the earth _ or lose a fight just to see _ you smile 'cause you got no flaws,
give a mil - lion dol - lars just for you to grab _ me by the col - lar and I'll come build us,

E5

no flaws. _____
build us. _____

I'm not

B

tryin' to be _ your part - time lov - er.

A

Sign me up _ for that full - time, I'm yours,

E5

I'm yours. _____

N.C.

So, what a man got - ta

STUCK WITH U

Words and Music by ARIANA GRANDE,
JUSTIN BIEBER, GIAN STONE,
WHITNEY PHILLIPS, FREDDY WEXLER,
SKYLER STONESTREET and SCOOTER BRAUN

Laid-back Ballad

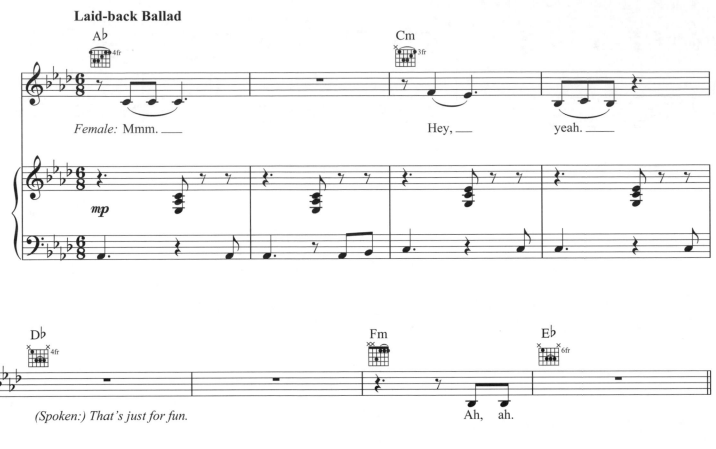

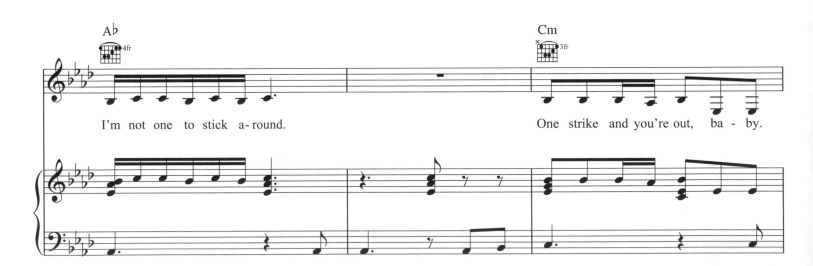

you.

Stuck with you, stuck with you, stuck with you.

SUNDAY BEST

Words and Music by FORREST FRANK
and COLIN PADALECKI

CONTEMPORARY HITS
FOR PIANO, VOICE AND GUITAR

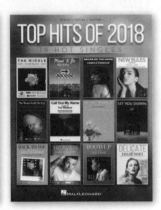

40 MOST STREAMED SONGS OF 2017-2018

40 of the Internet's most popular songs arranged for piano, voice and guitar. Includes: Despacito (Luis Fonsi & Daddy Yankee feat. Justin Bieber) • Feel It Still (Portugal. The Man) • New Rules (Dua Lipa) • Perfect (Ed Sheeran) • Wolves (Selena Gomez & Marshmello) • Young, Dumb and Broke (Khalid) • and more.
00283644 .... $19.99

CHART HITS OF 2019-2020

18 top singles arranged for piano and voice with guitar chords and lyrics. Songs include: Circles (Post Malone) • Dance Monkey (Tones and I) • Everything I Wanted (Billie Eilish) • Lose You to Love Me (Selena Gomez) • Lover (Taylor Swift) • Truth Hurts (Lizzo) • and more.
00334217 .... $17.99

Chart Hits of 2018-2019

18 of the hottest hits of '18 and '19, arranged for piano, voice and guitar. Includes: Eastside (Benny Blanco with Halsey & Khalid) • High Hopes (Panic! At the Disco) • Shallow (Lady Gaga & Bradley Cooper) • Sunflower (Post Malone & Swae Lee) • Without Me (Halsey) • and more.
00289816 .... $17.99

CONTEMPORARY R&B HITS

This collection pays tribute to two dozen of the best modern hits. Includes: All the Stars (Kendrick Lamar/SZA) • Girl on Fire (Alicia Keys/Nicki Minaj) • Love on the Brain (Rihanna) • Redbone (Childish Gambino) • and more.
00276001 .... $17.99

EDM SHEET MUSIC COLLECTION

37 hits from the EDM genre includes: Closer (The Chainsmokers feat. Halsey) • It Ain't Me (Kygo & Selena Gomez) • The Middle (Zedd, Maren Morris & Grey) • This Is What You Came For (Calvin Harris feat. Rihanna) • Titanium (David Guetta feat. Sia) • Wake Me Up! (Avicii) • and more.
00280949 .... $19.99

LATIN POP HITS

25 hot contemporary Latin songs including: Ahora Dice (Chris Jeday) • Bailando (Enrique Iglesias) • Despacito (Luis Fonsi & Daddy Yankee) • Échame La Culpa (Luis Fonsi & Demi Lovato) • Havana (Camila Cabello) • La Tortura (Shakira) • Súbeme La Radio (Enrique Iglesias) • and more.
00276076 .... $17.99

Order today from your favorite music retailer

HAL•LEONARD®
www.halleonard.com

POP HITS

You get a lot of bang for your bucks with this great collection of 52 top pop hits for only $14.99! Features: Believer • Blank Space • Despacito • Fight Song • HandClap • Lost Boy • Love Yourself • The Middle • One Call Away • Say Something • Send My Love (To Your New Lover) • 24K Magic • Wake Me Up • and more.
00289154 .... $14.99

POPULAR SHEET MUSIC – 30 HITS FROM 2017-2019

Play your favorite contemporary hits with this collection. Includes 30 songs: Bad Liar • Good As Hell • Havana • If I Can't Have You • Lover • The Middle • New Rules • Shallow • Shape of You • Sucker • Without Me • You Are the Reason • and more.
00345915 .... $19.99

TOP HITS OF 2018

18 of the best from '18 are included in this collection for piano, voice and guitar. Includes: Delicate (Taylor Swift) • In My Blood (Shawn Mendes) • Let You Down (NF) • The Middle (Zedd, Maren Morris & Grey) • New Rules (Dua Lipa) • No Tears Left to Cry (Ariana Grande) • and more.
00283394 .... $17.99

TOP HITS OF 2019

20 of the year's best are included in this collection. Includes: Bad Guy (Billie Eilish) • Dancing with a Stranger (Sam Smith & Normani) • ME! (Taylor Swift feat. Brendon Urie) • Old Town Road (Remix) (Lil Nas X feat. Billy Ray Cyrus) • Senorita (Shawn Mendes & Camila Cabello) • 7 Rings (Ariana Grande) • and more.
00302271 .... $17.99

Prices, contents, and availability subject to change without notice.